15.65

WEDDLE's
WIZNotes

Women Professionals Web-Sites

The Expert's Guide to the Best Job Boards for Finding Your Dream Job

Edited by Lindsey Chamberlain

ISBN: 1-928734-38-3

Special discounts on bulk quantities of WEDDLE's books are available for libraries, corporations, professional associations and other organizations. For details, please contact WEDDLE's at 203.964.1888.

WEDDLE's
www.weddles.com
2052 Shippan Avenue
Stamford, CT 06902
Where People Matter Most

*"Restaurant patrons
looking for quality dining have Zagat.
For the recruitment industry,
the name is Weddle ...
Peter Weddle that is."*

—American Staffing Association

The WEDDLE's
WIZNotes Series

Engineering Web Sites

Finance & Accounting Web Sites

Human Resource Web Sites

Managers & Executives Web Sites

Recent Graduate Web Sites

Sales & Marketing Web Sites

Scientist Web Sites

Women Professionals Web Sites

Finding a Job on the Web

Writing a Great Resume

**To order,
call 203.964.1888 or visit
www.weddles.com**

What is a WIZNotes?

A WIZNotes is your quick guide to the 40,000+ job boards and career portals now operating on the Internet. It provides the fast facts you need to determine which of those sites will best help you to find:

- a new or better job that will advance your career,

  or

- great talent for the open positions you have to fill in your organization.

Think of WIZNotes as a road map to employment resources on the Internet. Each volume in the series spotlights those sites on the Information Superhighway that offer information and services related to a specific occupational field or career situation. These services can include recruitment advertising (job postings), a resume database, a job agent and other features that would be helpful to job seekers and/or recruiters.

Each WIZNotes includes two types of sites:

- Those niche sites that specialize in the occupational field or career situation the WIZNotes covers

  and

- Those general purpose sites that have also reported significant activity in that occupational field or career situation.

For example, the WIZNotes for Sales and Marketing professionals includes Yahoo! HotJobs, a general purpose job board with significant job postings and visitor traffic in the sales and marketing field, and AllRetailJobs.com, a niche site that specializes in retail sales opportunities.

WHO CAN USE WIZNOTES?

If you're looking for a new or better job:

- Recent graduates
- Mid-career professionals
- Executives and managers in transition
- Those seeking to change their career field
- Military veterans entering the private sector
- Those re-entering the workforce after taking time off to raise children or acquire additional education
- Anyone who wants to advance their career and be the best they can be.

If you're searching for top notch talent:

- Corporate recruiters and employment managers
- Staffing firm recruiters and sourcing specialists
- Executive search consultants and head-hunters.

Currently, there are seven different volumes in the WEDDLE's WIZNotes series. They cover the following occupational fields or career situations:

- Engineers
- Executives and Managers
- Finance & Accounting Professionals
- Sales and Marketing Professionals
- Recent College Graduates
- Human Resource Professionals
- Scientists

Why use WIZNotes? Because they respect your time and accelerate your success. There is no extraneous information, and there are no extra pages. You get all that is required—and nothing more—to pick the job boards and career portals that will work best for you.

WHAT'S IN A WIZNOTES?

Each of the job boards and career portals listed in a WIZNotes is described with the following information:

* The site's name
* The site's Universal Research Locator (URL) or address on the Internet
* A picture of the site's home page on the Internet
* The date the site was founded
* The geographic coverage of the site (i.e., the countries it serves)
* Whether the site posts job openings
* Whether the site has a database of candidate resumes and/or profiles
* Whether the site offers a job agent
* The site's own description of its services and features. [Note: Site descriptions are edited for clarity and grammatical correctness.]

HOW IS THE INFORMATION IN A WIZNOTES COLLECTED?

The information that appears in a WIZNotes was obtained through WEDDLE's on-going site research and by visiting each Web-site. It is as accurate and current as we can make it. The Internet changes quickly, however, so we provide free, continuous updates of site information in the Free Book Updates area on the WEDDLE's Web site (www.weddles.com).

WHY IS THIS INFORMATION IMPORTANT TO YOU?

If you're a job seeker or career activist:

INFORMATION	IMPORTANCE TO YOU
The site's name	Enables you to use a search engine such as Google.com or Yahoo! to look for other information about and reviews of the site's performance.
The site's address on the Internet	Visiting the site will help you determine whether it is well maintained and professionally operated.
A picture of the site's Home Page	Gives you a sense of the site's look and feel before you visit.
The date the site was founded	Generally, the longer a site has been in operation, the more established its services and reliable its performance.
The geographic coverage of the site	Indicates whether the site's services will help you find employment opportunities where you live or want to.
Whether the site posts job openings	Tells you if there are job ads for you to review on the site.
Whether the site has a database of resumes or profiles	Tells you if you can store a resume or employment profile on the site.
Whether the site offers a job agent	Tells you if you can sign up for this free feature which automatically compares your specified employment objective with jobs posted on the site and privately notifies you of matches.
The site's self-description	Provides additional information about the site's services, features and fees.

If you're a recruiter or HR professional:

INFORMATION	IMPORTANCE TO YOU
The site's name	Enables you to use a search engine such as Google.com or Yahoo! to look for other information about and reviews of the site's performance.
The site's address on the Internet	Visiting the site will help you determine whether it is well maintained and professionally operated.
A picture of the site's Home Page	Gives you a sense of the site's look and feel before you visit.
The date the site was founded	Generally, the longer a site has been in operation, the more established its services and reliable its performance.
The geographic coverage of the site	Indicates whether the site's services can used where your openings are located.
Whether the site posts job openings	Tells you if you can post job openings on the site.
Whether the site has a database of resumes or profiles	Tells you if you can search candidate resumes and/or profiles on the site.
Whether the site offers a job agent	Tells you if the site provides this job search service that also protects a person's confidentiality and thus increases the site's appeal to passive prospects.
The site's self-description	Provides additional information about the site's services, features and fees.

WHY INCLUDE SITES
THAT DON'T POST JOBS
OR OFFER A RESUME DATABASE?

A WIZNotes provides information on two kinds of sites: job boards and career portals. While the former always include a listing of employment opportunities and often a resume/profile database, the latter sometimes does not. Nevertheless, career portals are often very helpful to both job seekers and recruiters.

For job seekers, career portals can offer access to professional or industry knowledge, continuing education and other developmental opportunities and networking venues. For recruiters, they offer information and insight on a particular profession, craft, trade or industry and a way to network with individuals who are active in and committed to their career field.

HOW DO YOU USE A WIZNOTES?

The following five steps will help you use the information in your WIZNotes effectively:

STEP 1: Scan all of the sites contained in your WIZNotes and identify the 10-12 sites that seem to best serve your employment/ recruitment objective.

STEP 2: Use the detailed information provided in each site profile to compare those 10-12 sites and select your 6-8 best options.

STEP 3: Visit the 6-8 sites and evaluate their look and feel, performance, and customer service.

STEP 4: Select 3-5 finalists and put them to work for you.

STEP 5: Every six months or so, repeat this process to ensure that the sites you selected are providing the level of support you deserve.

WHAT IS WEDDLE'S?

WEDDLE's is a research and publishing company that specializes in the employment resources on the Internet. Since 1996, its print publications have been the leading source of information for both job seekers and recruiters. WEDDLE's Guides and Directories are published annually and have earned an international reputation for accuracy and helpfulness. They are sold in major bookstores nationwide and through the online Catalog at the WEDDLE's Website, www.weddles.com.

YOUR NOTES

The Sites in Your WIZNotes

Advancing Women
American Association of University Women
American Business Women's Association
American Medical Women's Association
American Women's Society of Certified Public Accountants
Association for Women in Computing
Association for Women Geoscientists
Association of Women Industrial Designers
Association for Women in Mathematics
Association of Women Professionals
Association for Women in Science
Association for Women's Rights in Development
BellaOnline
Black Career Women
BlueSuitMom.com
CareerBabe
CareerBuilder.com
career-intelligence.com
CareerWomen.com
Catalyst
Center for Women and Information Technology
CineWomen
Coalition of Labor Union Women
DC Web Women
Dress for Success
Empower Me!
eWorkingWomen.com
Executive Women in Government
Feminist Majority Foundation
Financial Women International, Inc.
Financial Women's Association

ForHerSuccess.com
GirlGeeks
IMDiversity.com
Institution of Women in Trades, Technology and
   Science/WomenTechWorld.org
Journalism and Women Symposium
LIWomen.com
MomMD.com
Monster.com
MoviesByWomen.com
National Association for Female Executives
National Association of Insurance Women
National Association of Women in Construction
National Women's Law Center
National Women's Studies Association
9to5: National Association of Working Women
Organization of Women in International Trade
Society of Canadian Women in Science and Technology
Society of Women Engineers
Tradeswomen, Inc.
U.S. Women's Chamber of Commerce
WomanOwned.com
Womans-Work.com
Women Executives in Public Relations
Women on the Fast Track
Women in Higher Education
Women For Hire
Women in Neuroscience
Women in Packaging, Inc.
Women in Sports Careers
WomenSportsJobs.com
Women in Technology International
Women Unlimited

Women Work!
Women's Environmental Council
WomensJobList.com
WomensMedia
Women's Work
Work4Women
Working Moms Refuge
WorldWIT (Women-Insights-Technology)
WWWomen.com
Yahoo! HotJobs
Yummy Mummy Careers

Please choose your sites carefully. The inclusion of a site in a WEDDLE's WIZNotes is not an endorsement or recommendation of the site by WEDDLE's or Peter Weddle.

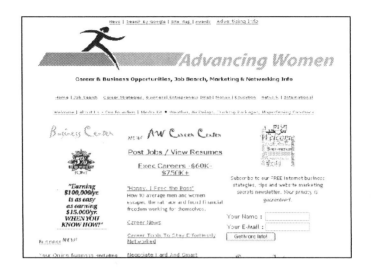

Advancing Women
www.advancingwomen.com

Date Founded:	1996
Geographic Coverage:	USA and Canada
Job Board:	Yes
Resume Database:	Yes
Job Agent:	Yes

Description: Advancing Women's goal is to help women define and empower themselves as professional and businesswomen. Advancing Women gives users not only the information and strategies needed but the actual tools to support women in their goal of success. Advancing Women offers a Career Center where employment recruiters who are looking for women and minorities can interface with users who are seeking better pay and more promising careers.

Your Notes

www.weddles.com

American Association of University Women (AAUW)
www.aauw.org/about/jobmarket.cfm

Date Founded:	1881
Geographic Coverage:	USA
Job Board:	Yes
Resume Database:	No
Job Agent:	No

Description: For more than a century, the American Association of University Women (AAUW) has been the nationís leading voice promoting education and equity for women and girls. Through its vital nationwide network, AAUW opens doors for women and girls and influences public debate on critical social issues such as education, civil rights, and health care. AAUW's Career Center includes updated job listings in university settings.

Your Notes

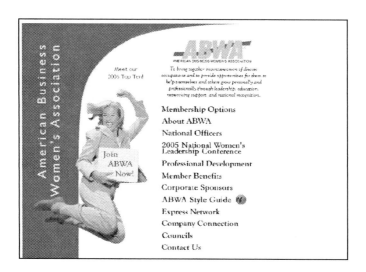

American Business Women's Association (ABWA)
www.abwahq.org

Date Founded:	1949
Geographic Coverage:	USA
Job Board:	No
Resume Database:	No
Job Agent:	No

Description: The American Business Women's Association (ABWA) has long been accepted as one of the leading business womenís associations in the United States, and its far-reaching influence has touched the lives and careers of many. Tens of thousands of members gather throughout the country, united by a common goaló to support each other in professional development and career advancement.

Your Notes

American Medical Women's Association (AMWA)

www.amwa-doc.org

Date Founded:	1915
Geographic Coverage:	International
Job Board:	Yes
Resume Database:	Yes
Job Agent:	Yes

Description: For the past 90 years, the American Medical Women's Association (AMWA) has served as the vision and voice of women in medicine. AMWA has provided support for female physicians since 1915, a time when women doctors were a rarity. AMWAís new Career Center allows job seekers to search over 1.3 million jobs, and offers solutions for changing jobs, resume writing and interviewing, while also allowing employers to post jobs online easily and search resumes from qualified candidates.

Your Notes

American Women's Society of Certified Public Accountants (AWSCPA)
www.awscpa.org

Date Founded: 1933
Geographic Coverage: USA
Job Board: Yes
Resume Database: Yes
Job Agent: No

Description: The American Woman's Society of Certified Public Accountants (AWSCPA) is a national organization dedicated to serving all women CPAs. The AWSCPA provides a supportive environment and valuable resources for members to achieve their personal and professional goals through various opportunities including leadership, networking. education, and online employment assistance.

Your Notes

www.weddles.com

Association for
Women in Computing (AWC)
www.awc-hq.org

Date Founded:	1978
Geographic Coverage:	USA
Job Board:	No
Resume Database:	No
Job Agent:	No

Description: The Association for Women in Computing (AWC) is a not-for-profit, professional organization for individuals with an interest in information technology. AWC is dedicated to the advancement of women in the computing fields, in business, industry, science, education, government, and the military. AWC's purpose is to provide opportunities for professional growth through networking and through programs on technical and career-oriented topics. One benefit of membership is access to job listings through our local chapters.

Your Notes

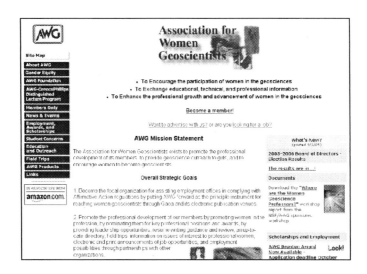

Association for
Women Geoscientists (AWG)
www.awg.org

Date Founded:	1977
Geographic Coverage:	International
Job Board:	Yes
Resume Database:	No
Job Agent:	No

Description: The Association for Women Geoscientists (AWG) is an international organization devoted to enhancing the quality and level of participation of women in the geosciences and to introducing girls and young women to geoscience careers. Membersí diverse interests and expertise cover the entire spectrum of geoscience disciplines and career paths, providing a variety of networking and mentoring opportunities.

Your Notes

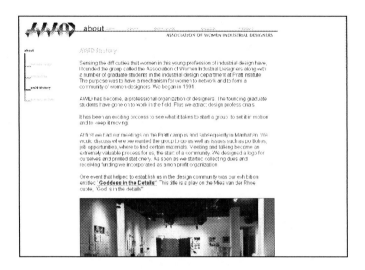

Association of
Women Industrial Designers (AWID)
www.awidweb.com

Date Founded:	1991
Geographic Coverage:	International
Job Board:	Yes
Resume Database:	No
Job Agent:	No

Description: The Association of Women Industrial Designers (AWID) is an international resource that facilitates access to design talent, networking, and social interaction in the design community. AWID provides a forum for publicizing the work of members and for the dissemination of current design news and information, including current job listings.

Your Notes

Association for
Women in Mathematics (AWM)
www.awm-math.org/career.html

Date Founded:	1971
Geographic Coverage:	International
Job Board:	Yes
Resume Database:	No
Job Agent:	No

Description: The Association for Women in Mathematics (AWM) is a non-profit organization founded in 1971. Its continuing goal is to encourage women in the mathematical sciences. AWM currently has members representing a broad spectrum of the mathematical communityó from the United States and around the world. AWM's career resources include electronic job ads and employment resources, articles about careers in the mathematical sciences, and links to more resources for women in math.

Your Notes

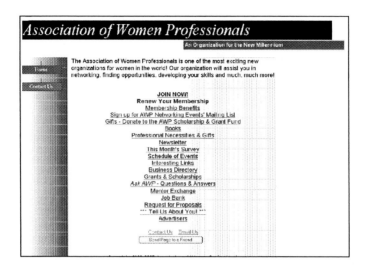

Association of Women Professionals
www.awoman.org

Date Founded:	2000
Geographic Coverage:	USA
Job Board:	Yes
Resume Database:	No
Job Agent:	No

Description: The Association of Women Professionals is an exciting new organization for women. It assists women in networking, developing new skills, and finding professional opportunities. Available on the association's Web-site is a question and answer section for business and career issues as well as a mentor exchange program in which members and mentors are matched based on specific expertise and experience. The site also offers a job bank where current job listings across the United States are posted.

Your Notes

Association for Women in Science (AWIS)
www.awis.org

Date Founded:	1971
Geographic Coverage:	USA
Job Board:	Yes
Resume Database:	No
Job Agent:	No

Description: The Association for Women in Science (AWIS) is dedicated to achieving equity and full participation for women in science, mathematics, engineering and technology. As part of its efforts to promote the entrance and advancement of women in science, AWIS has a long-standing commitment to fostering the careers of women science professionals, from mentoring to scholarships to job listings.

Your Notes

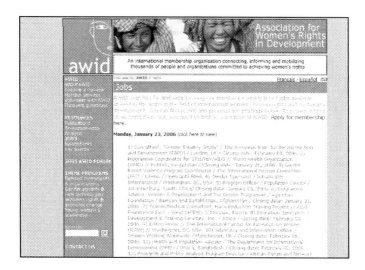

Association for
Women's Rights in Development
(AWID)
www.awid.org/jobs

Date Founded:	1982
Geographic Coverage:	International
Job Board:	Yes
Resume Database:	No
Job Agent:	No

Description: The Association for Women's Rights in Development (AWID) is an international membership organization connecting, informing, and mobilizing people and organizations committed to achieving gender equality, sustainable development and women's human rights. AWID searches far and wide to bring its members a weekly list of jobs available around the world in the field of international women's human rights and sustainable development.

Your Notes

www.weddles.com

BellaOnline
www.bellaonline.com

Date Founded:	1999
Geographic Coverage:	USA
Job Board:	No
Resume Database:	No
Job Agent:	No

Description: BellaOnline, "the voice of women," provides an encouraging, supportive publishing community for women. This community provides free training, support and promotion so writers may reach their personal and business goals. Overall, BellaOnline aims to provide high-quality, helpful, trustworthy content, at no cost, in a low advertisement environment for millions of women. The career section of BellaOnline provides readers with advice, resources, and informative articles about changing careers and developing professionally.

Your Notes

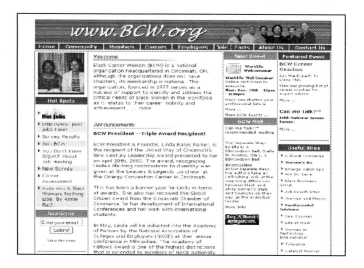

Black Career Women (BCW)

www.bcw.org

Date Founded:	1977
Geographic Coverage:	USA
Job Board:	Yes
Resume Database:	Yes
Job Agent:	No

Description: Black Career Women (BCW) serves to identify and address the critical needs of black women in the workforce. BCW's members are diverse, representing women workers from entry level to the executive suite. As well as being a resource for job seekers, BCW's Web-site is visited by employers searching for black women to meet their diversity hiring needs, community groups attempting to expand the involvement of black women with their organizations, executive search firms, and women seeking mentors or connections with other career-concerned women.

Your Notes

BlueSuitMom.com
www.bluesuitmom.com

Date Founded:	2000
Geographic Coverage:	International
Job Board:	Yes
Resume Database:	Yes
Job Agent:	Yes

Description: BlueSuitMom.com is the premier resource of work and family balance information for executive working mothers and their employers. The site includes advice on parenting, career advancement, the balancing act, meal planning and family health and fitness, delivered in a format that nurtures respect for professional mothers. BlueSuitMom's career section offers articles and resources for finding balance and changing jobs, support for women-owned business, and an online job center.

Your Notes

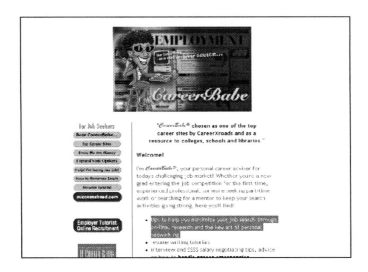

CareerBabe
www.careerbabe.com

Date Founded:	1995
Geographic Coverage:	USA
Job Board:	No
Resume Database:	No
Job Agent:	No

Description: CareerBabe acts as a personal career adviser for today's challenging job market. The site provides tips to help maximize job searches through on-line research and the key art of personal networking, resume writing tutorials, interview and salary negotiating tips, and career transition information and resources. The creator of CareerBabe´ Fran Quittel´ is experienced in Internet/Intranet recruiting, issues involving job seekers, employer online recruitment decisions and many facets of the electronic recruitment marketplace.

Your Notes

www.weddles.com

CareerBuilder.com
www.careerbuilder.com

Date Founded:	1996
Geographic Coverage:	USA
Job Board:	Yes
Resume Database:	Yes
Job Agent:	Yes

Description: At CareerBuilder, we realize that every minute you save brings you a minute closer to landing the perfect job. You can post and manage up to 5 different resumes, apply online when you find the right job, and be assured that your resume can be read by today's online hiring software! In addition, by using our "Save this Search" feature, you can get right back into the job hunt without duplicating efforts each time you sign in.

Your Notes

www.weddles.com

career-intelligence.com
www.career-intelligence.com

Date Founded:	2000
Geographic Coverage:	International
Job Board:	Yes
Resume Database:	Yes
Job Agent:	Yes

Description: Career-intelligence.com is a by-women, for-women career resource with a philosophy of stretch, grow, achieve. The mission of career-intelligence.com is to help women achieve personal and professional satisfaction by providing the information, support and tools needed to succeed in today's competitive economy. The creators of career-intelligence.com aim to help women find the jobs that are right for them and assist them through all the different phases of their careers.

Your Notes

CareerWomen.com
www.careerwomen.com

Date Founded:	1996
Geographic Coverage:	International
Job Board:	Yes
Resume Database:	Yes
Job Agent:	No

Description: CareerWomen.com is a member of The Career Exposure Network. This network is a 100% women-owned e-recruiting network of premier niche sites that have been helping employers find top quality candidates to meet their growing business needs since 1996. The Career Exposure Network is dedicated to helping its network-wide job candidates find the best career opportunities with the best companies while helping its employers further their e-recruiting efforts.

Your Notes

www.weddles.com

Catalyst

www.catalystwomen.org

Date Founded:	1962
Geographic Coverage:	International
Job Board:	No
Resume Database:	No
Job Agent:	No

Description: Catalyst is the leading research and advisory organization working with businesses and the professions to build inclusive environments and expand opportunities for women at work. As an independent, nonprofit membership organization, Catalyst conducts research on all aspects of womenís career advancement and provides strategic and Web-based consulting services globally.

Your Notes

www.weddles.com

Center for
Women and Information Technology
(CWIT)
www.umbc.edu/cwit

Date Founded: 1998
Geographic Coverage: USA
Job Board: No
Resume Database: No
Job Agent: No

Description: The Center for Women and Information Technology (CWIT) is dedicated to providing global leadership in achieving women's full participation in all aspects of information technology (IT). Women's participation in IT will strengthen the workforce, raise the standard of living for many women, and help to assure that information technology addresses women's needs and expands the possibilities for their lives.

Your Notes

CineWomen
www.cinewomen.org

Date Founded:	1990
Geographic Coverage:	Regional-USA: NY, CA
Job Board:	No
Resume Database:	No
Job Agent:	No

Description: CineWomen is a member-run, nonprofit organization of women in the film, television, and re-lated arts and industries, whose purpose is supporting the advancement of women, their goals, and their visions in a non-competitive environment. CineWomen is dedi-cated to providing a secure forum for our members to meet and grow, to developing the number and range of opportunities available in the cinematic industries, and to fostering a strong, independent, creative spirit.

Your Notes

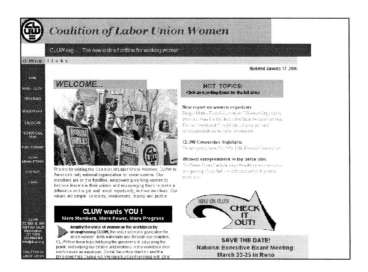

Coalition of
Labor Union Women (CLUW)
www.cluw.org

Date Founded: 1974
Geographic Coverage: USA and Canada
Job Board: No
Resume Database: No
Job Agent: No

Description: The Coalition of Labor Union Women (CLUW) is America's only national organization for unionized women. The primary mission of CLUW is to unify all union women in a viable organization to determine their common problems and concerns, and to develop action programs within the framework of unions to deal effectively with CLUW's objectives.

Your Notes

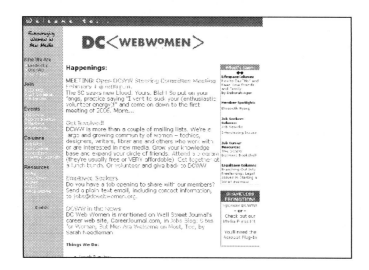

DC Web Women

www.dcwebwomen.org

Date Founded:	1995
Geographic Coverage:	Regional-USA: WDC
Job Board:	No
Resume Database:	Yes
Job Agent:	No

Description: DC Web Women is a non-profit professional organization for women that provides opportunities to educate, learn, network, and serve the Washington, DC community. DC Web Women strives to create role models for young women and girls and to promote women in technology. Our mission is to provide a forum for women involved or interested in new media. Subscribers' resumes are posted to our mailing list.

Your Notes

Dress for Success
www.dressforsuccess.org

Date Founded:	1996
Geographic Coverage:	International
Job Board:	No
Resume Database:	No
Job Agent:	No

Description: Dress for Success is a not-for-profit organization that offers services to help clients enter the workforce and stay employed. The mission of Dress for Success is to advance low-income women's economic and social development and to encourage self-sufficiency through career development and employment retention. Dress for Success provides programs that help economically disadvantaged women acquire jobs, retain their new positions and succeed in the mainstream workplace.

Your Notes

Empower Me!
www.empowerme.org

Date Founded:	1998
Geographic Coverage:	USA
Job Board:	Yes
Resume Database:	Yes
Job Agent:	No

Description: Empower Me! is one of the top resources for African American professional and business women and companies concerned with initiatives for the advancement of African American women in the workplace. Empower Me! provides a host of services to companies, business women and career women including coaching, business development consulting, executive recruiting, specialty career fairs, career transition consulting, e-learning (online courses), workshops, mentor matching, and networking.

Your Notes

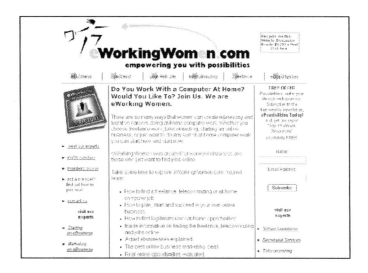

eWorkingWomen.com
www.eworkingwomen.com

Date Founded: 2000
Geographic Coverage: USA
Job Board: No
Resume Database: No
Job Agent: No

Description: eWorkingWomen.com was created for women in business and those who just want to find jobs online. Our site helps women find freelance, telecommuting, or at-home computer jobs and gives expert advice on how to plan, start, and succeed in your own home-based business. We also provide intro-ductions to a range of business topics and opportunities, answers to the most common questions, and related links and resources.

Your Notes

Executive Women in Government (EWG)

www.execwomeningov.org

Date Founded: 1974
Geographic Coverage: USA
Job Board: No
Resume Database: No
Job Agent: No

Description: Executive Women in Government (EWG) is a nonprofit professional organization of women employed by the Federal government at senior or executive levels. EWG is a powerful force for advancing women in senior leadership positions in Federal government. The primary goal of EWG is to promote, support and mentor women for senior leadership positions in the Federal government.

Your Notes

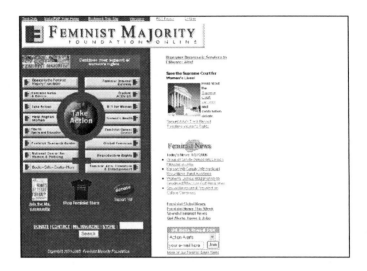

Feminist Majority Foundation (FMF)
www.feminist.org

Date Founded:	1987
Geographic Coverage:	International
Job Board:	Yes
Resume Database:	Yes
Job Agent:	No

Description: The Feminist Majority Foundation (FMF) is a cutting edge organization dedicated to women's equality, reproductive health, and non-violence. To carry out these aims, FMF engages in research and public policy development, public education programs, grassroots organizing projects, and leadership training and development programs. The Feminist Career Center has full-time, part-time, and internship positions at feminist and progressive organizations across the United States and the world.

Your Notes

Financial Women International, Inc. (FWI)

www.fwi.org

Date Founded:	1921
Geographic Coverage:	USA
Job Board:	Yes
Resume Database:	Yes
Job Agent:	Yes

Description: Financial Women International (FWI) is a professional organization of women who seek to expand their personal and professional capabilities and support the development of others. FWI's members represent a diversity of occupations in or supporting the financial services industry. Financial Women International's Career Center offers a focused job search engine for financial services careers.

Your Notes

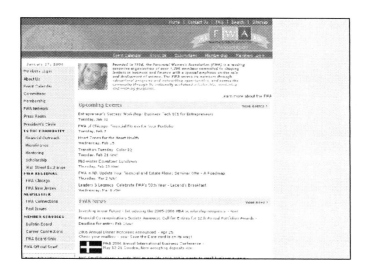

Financial Women's Association (FWA)

www.fwa.org

Date Founded: 1956
Geographic Coverage: USA
Job Board: Yes
Resume Database: No
Job Agent: No

Description: The Financial Women's Association (FWA) is a leading executive organization of over 1,200 members committed to shaping leaders in business and finance with a special emphasis on the role and development of women. The FWA offers its members educational programs and networking opportunities. Members also have confidential access to employment listings.

Your Notes

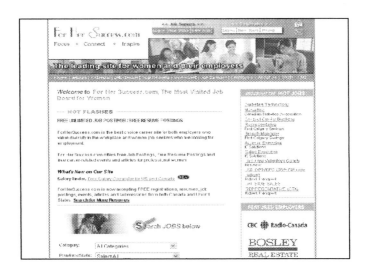

ForHerSuccess.com
www.forhersuccess.com

Date Founded:	2003
Geographic Coverage:	Regional-Canada: GTA
Job Board:	Yes
Resume Database:	Yes
Job Agent:	No

Description: ForHerSuccess.com strives to be the most recognized Internet career management center for professional women in the greater Toronto area. With a keen interest in the advancement of professional women, ForHerSuccess.com acts as an Internet employment Web-site, delivering premier employment services to companies seeking pre-screened professional help and a resource for professional women looking for a new position.

Your Notes

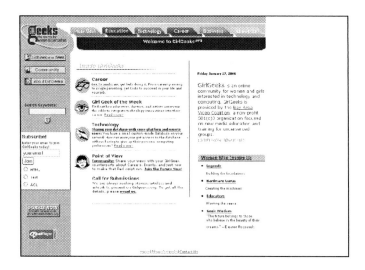

GirlGeeks
www.girlgeeks.org

Date Founded:	1998
Geographic Coverage:	USA
Job Board:	No
Resume Database:	No
Job Agent:	No

Description: GirlGeeks is an online community for women and girls interested in technology and computing. GirlGeeks' Career Center includes career tips, life and success strategies, suggested reading, surveys, career news, and links and resources for people looking for new jobs or trying to advance their existing careers. These resources include a list of job boards, career seminar and workshop information, and workplace and women's rights resources.

Your Notes

IMDiversity.com
www.imdiversity.com

Date Founded:	1970
Geographic Coverage:	International
Job Board:	Yes
Resume Database:	Yes
Job Agent:	Yes

Description: IMDiversity.com was conceived by *The Black Collegian Magazine*, which has provided African-American college students with valuable information on career and job opportunities since 1970. The site is dedicated to providing career and self-development information to all minorities. IMDiversity.com strives to provide access to the largest database of equal opportunity employers committed to workplace diversity.

Your Notes

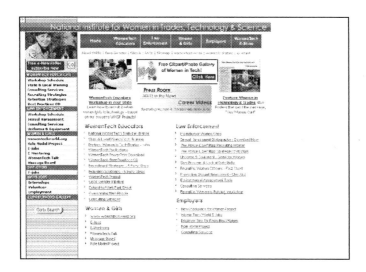

Institution for Women in Trades, Technology, and Science (IWITTS) WomenTechWorld.org

www.iwitts.com

www.womentechworld.org

Date Founded:	1994
Geographic Coverage:	USA
Job Board:	Yes
Resume Database:	No
Job Agent:	Yes

Description: The Institution for Women in Trades, Technology, and Science (IWITTS) provides the tools to successfully integrate women into male-dominated careers. IWITTS worked on a national level to develop WomenTechWorld.org, an online community for women technicians to connect with each other. The site features several interactive areas designed to facilitate peer support among women in technology.

Your Notes

www.weddles.com

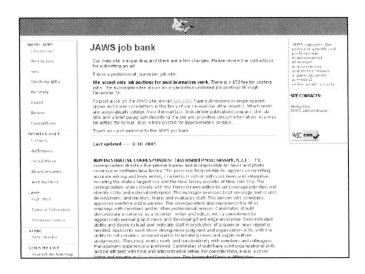

Journalism and Women Symposium (JAWS)

www.jaws.org/jobs/index.shtml

Date Founded:	1985
Geographic Coverage:	International
Job Board:	Yes
Resume Database:	No
Job Agent:	No

Description: The Journalism and Women Symposium (JAWS) brings together women journalists and journalism educators and researchers from across the country, and sometimes the world, to meet in an atmosphere of mutual support and professional growth. JAWS supports the personal growth and professional empowerment of women in newsrooms and works toward a more accurate portrayal of the whole society.

Your Notes

www.weddles.com

LIWomen.com
www.liwomen.com

Date Founded:	2000
Geographic Coverage:	Regional-USA: NY
Job Board:	No
Resume Database:	No
Job Agent:	No

Description: LIWomen.com is the online resource for the women of Long Island. The group's mission is to provide information on self-development, self-discovery, and issues affecting the lives of women in the Long Island community. LIWomen.com has been featured as a resource where women can access information on self-development and self-discovery, as well as a place to turn for information on seminars, business, health, spirituality, and other issues that affect women on a daily basis.

Your Notes

www.weddles.com

MomMD.com
www.mommd.com

Date Founded:	1999
Geographic Coverage:	USA
Job Board:	Yes
Resume Database:	No
Job Agent:	No

Description: Start your job search at MomMD.com. Job listings include full-time, part-time, flex-time and job sharing opportunities nationwide. MomMD.com also includes resources to start, enhance, and develop your medical career. Doctors already in practice can find or advertise a job opportunity; learn about job sharing; find a physician job share partner; and use business-of-medicine resources. Students can find medical school admissions and medical education information, and learn what it takes to become a doctor.

Your Notes

Monster.com

www.monster.com

Date Founded:	1994
Geographic Coverage:	USA
Job Board:	Yes
Resume Database:	Yes
Job Agent:	Yes

Description: Monster.com allows job seekers to create their own online resume and application for submission to jobs online, and to have employers that have been screened through Monster.com find them using our system. In addition, Monster.com allows job seekers to receive e-mails about job notices matching their search criteria. For recruiters, whether you're looking for great local talent or conducting a nationwide search, Monster can help you find and hire the right people for your company.

Your Notes

MoviesByWomen.com
www.moviesbywomen.com

Date Founded:	2000
Geographic Coverage:	International
Job Board:	Yes
Resume Database:	No
Job Agent:	No

Description: MoviesByWomen.com was created to promote equality for women in film, television, and all other media. Two of the group's main goals are to increase the number of women directors working in film, television or other media and to develop a community that will increase employment opportunities for women in entertainment. The recently-created job board is open to those experienced in crew, production, and post-positions who would like to list either their services or a job opening. The board is updated monthly.

Your Notes

National Association for Female Executives (NAFE)

www.nafe.com

Date Founded:	1972
Geographic Coverage:	USA
Job Board:	Yes
Resume Database:	Yes
Job Agent:	Yes

Description: The National Association for Female Executives (NAFE) is one of the nationís largest businesswomenís associations with over 60,000 members, including 20,000 women business owners. NAFE provides resources and services through education, networking, and public advocacy to empower its members to achieve career success and financial security. NAFE is part of Working Mother Media, publisher of *Working Mother* magazine.

Your Notes

www.weddles.com

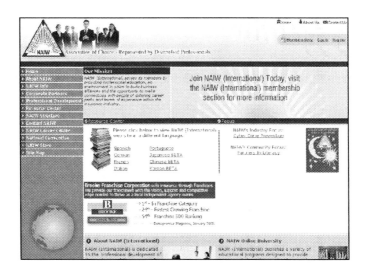

National Association of Insurance Women (NAIW)
www.naiw.org

Date Founded: 1940
Geographic Coverage: International
Job Board: Yes
Resume Database: Yes
Job Agent: No

Description: The National Association of Insurance Women (NAIW) serves its members by providing professional education, an environment in which to build business alliances and the opportunity to make connections with people of differing career paths and levels of experience within the insurance industry.

Your Notes

National Association of Women in Construction (NAWIC)

www.nawic.org

Date Founded:	1955
Geographic Coverage:	International
Job Board:	Yes
Resume Database:	Yes
Job Agent:	Yes

Description: The National Association of Women in Construction (NAWIC) was founded by 16 women working in the construction industry. Knowing that women represented only a small fraction of the construction industry, the founders organized NAWIC to create a support network. NAWIC has since grown to include 5,500 members. NAWIC's core purpose is to enhance the success of women in the construction industry.

Your Notes

National Women's Law Center (NWLC)
www.nwlc.org

Date Founded:	1972
Geographic Coverage:	USA
Job Board:	No
Resume Database:	No
Job Agent:	No

Description: The National Women's Law Center (NWLC) has expanded the possibilities for women and girls in this country. The Center uses the law in all its forms: getting new laws on the books and enforced; litigating ground-breaking cases in state and federal courts all the way to the Supreme Court; and educating the public about ways to make the law and public policies work for women and their families.

Your Notes

www.weddles.com

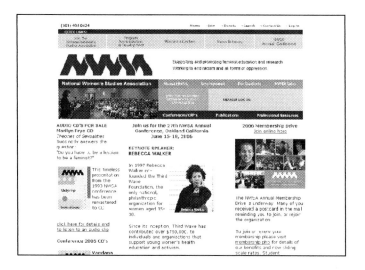

National Women's Studies Association (NWSA)
www.nwsa.org

Date Founded: 1977
Geographic Coverage: International
Job Board: Yes
Resume Database: No
Job Agent: No

Description: The National Women's Studies Association (NWSA) is committed to supporting and promoting feminist teaching, research, education, and professional and community service. The NWSA also works to end racism and all forms of oppression. International job postings include openings in women's studies, gender studies, and other academic departments as well as in campus centers, resource centers, and research institutions.

Your Notes

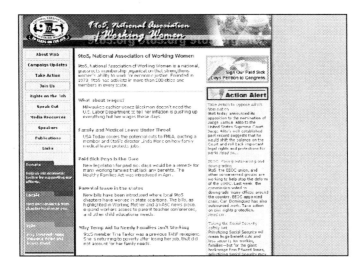

9to5: National Association of Working Women

www.9to5.org

Date Founded:	1973
Geographic Coverage:	USA
Job Board:	No
Resume Database:	No
Job Agent:	No

Description: 9to5, the National Association of Working Women, is a national, grassroots membership organization that strengthens women's ability to work for economic justice. 9to5 is committed to winning family-friendly policies to help working people balance responsibilities at home and on-the-job, making non-standard jobs voluntary and equitable, eliminating workplace discrimination, and opposing punitive welfare policies.

Your Notes

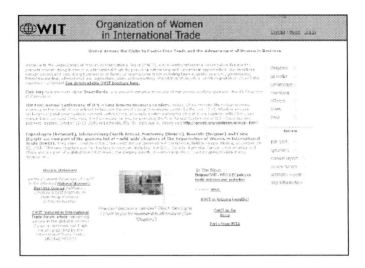

Organization of Women
in International Trade (OWIT)
www.owit.org

Date Founded:	1989
Geographic Coverage:	International
Job Board:	Yes
Resume Database:	No
Job Agent:	No

Description: The Organization of Women in International Trade (OWIT) is an organization created to promote women in international trade by providing networking and educational opportunities. OWIT's members include women and men doing business in all facets of international trade including finance, public relations, government, freight forwarding, international law, agriculture, sales and marketing, import/export, logistics, and transportation.

Your Notes

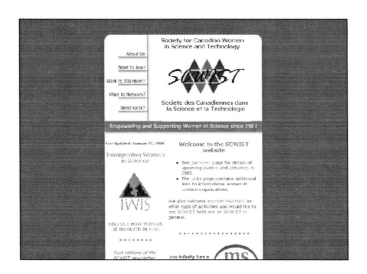

Society of Canadian Women in Science and Technology (SCWIST)
www.harbour.sfu.ca/scwist

Date Founded:	1981
Geographic Coverage:	Canada
Job Board:	No
Resume Database:	No
Job Agent:	No

Description: The Society of Canadian Women in Science and Technology (SCWIST) is a non-profit, voluntary association established to promote, encourage, and empower women working in science and technology. A major goal of SCWIST is to increase the representation, retention and status of women in the science and technology workplace by providing networking and mentoring opportunities.

Your Notes

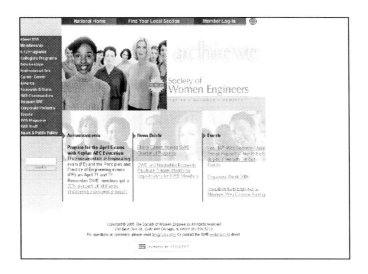

Society of Women Engineers (SWE)
www.swe.org

Date Founded:	1950
Geographic Coverage:	USA
Job Board:	Yes
Resume Database:	No
Job Agent:	No

Description: The Society of Women Engineers (SWE) is an educational and service organization. SWE empowers women to succeed and advance in their engineering aspirations and be recognized for their contributions as engineers and leaders. SWE strives to inform young women of the opportunities open to them, assist women in returning to active work after temporary retirement, serve as a center of information on women in engineering, and encourage women engineers to attain high levels of education and professional achievement.

Your Notes

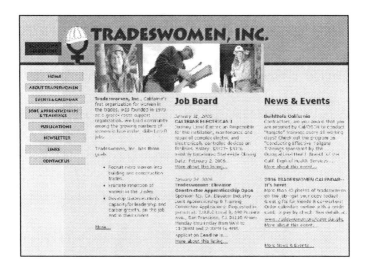

Tradeswomen, Inc.
www.tradeswomen.org

Date Founded:	1979
Geographic Coverage:	Regional-USA: CA
Job Board:	Yes
Resume Database:	No
Job Agent:	No

Description: Tradeswomen, Inc., California's first organization for women in the trades, was founded as a grassroots support group. Tradeswomen, Inc. builds community among the growing numbers of women in blue collar, skilled craft jobs. The organization has three goals: to recruit more women into building and construction trades, to promote retention of women in the trades, and to develop tradeswomen's capacity for leadership and career growth, on-the-job and in their unions. The organization provides listings for jobs, apprenticeships, and training programs.

Your Notes

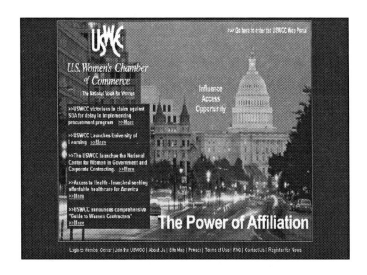

U.S. Women's Chamber of Commerce (USWCC)
www.sblink.us/html/uswcc.aspx

Date Founded:	2001
Geographic Coverage:	USA
Job Board:	Yes
Resume Database:	No
Job Agent:	No

Description: The U.S. Women's Chamber of Commerce (USWCC) has established a new standard of leadership for women. To increase the influence of women, USWCC is implementing important strategic shifts, focusing on targeted issues, providing education and awareness, and creating strong connections and advocacy. USWCC members have access to the National Women's Job Center, where women career professionals and graduates go to connect with new opportunities.

Your Notes

WomanOwned.com
www.womanowned.com

Date Founded:	1997
Geographic Coverage:	International
Job Board:	No
Resume Database:	No
Job Agent:	No

Description: By word of mouth, WomanOwned.com has grown to serve over 1.5 million women business owners from all around the world. WomanOwned.com provides online business information and networking assistance as well as a number of resources for setting up, running, and growing businesses. The site features an online search engine of women business owners from every type of industry and from almost every country around the world.

Your Notes

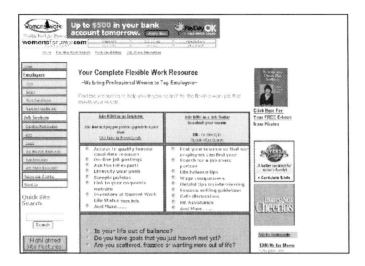

Womans-Work.com
www.womans-work.com

Date Founded:	2000
Geographic Coverage:	USA
Job Board:	Yes
Resume Database:	Yes
Job Agent:	No

Description: Womans-Work.com strives to help women find professional, flexible work situations. The organization brings qualified candidates to progressive companies and provides them with the tools and resources necessary to transform the design of their workplaces. The goal of Womans-Work.com is to increase the menu of choices available to women. Resources include links to family-friendly companies, job listings, and job sharing resources.

Your Notes

Women Executives in Public Relations (WEPR)

www.wepr.org/job_board.asp

Date Founded:	1945
Geographic Coverage:	USA
Job Board:	Yes
Resume Database:	No
Job Agent:	No

Description: Women Executives in Public Relations (WEPR) is the countryís premier membership organization for accomplished women in the public relations and marketing communications fields. WEPR membership provides an important career credential for PR practitioners. The new job board contains industry-related job openings nationwide and is open to members and non-members.

Your Notes

Women on the Fast Track
www.womenonthefasttrack.com

Date Founded:	1998
Geographic Coverage:	USA
Job Board:	No
Resume Database:	Yes
Job Agent:	No

Description: Women on the Fast Track is a rapidly growing, nationally known networking organization for business and professional women. Originating in New York City, Women on the Fast Track has established chapters in several states. The members of Women on the Fast Track make the organization successful. Committed to their businesses, their professions, and to each other, the members of each group meet monthly. Each chapter is comprised of 10-15 women, all unique to their group, yet each sharing a common awareness: that networking is essential to their success.

Your Notes

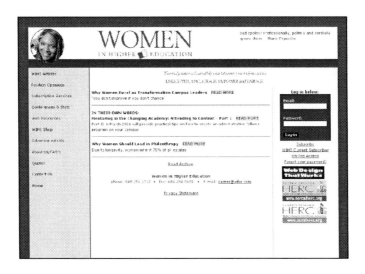

Women in Higher Education (WIHE)
www.wihe.com

Date Founded: 1992
Geographic Coverage: International
Job Board: Yes
Resume Database: No
Job Agent: No

Description: Women in Higher Education (WIHE) is a monthly practitionerís news journal, designed to help women on campus learn about how gender affects their being successful in the male-dominated world of higher education. Its goals are to enlighten, encourage, empower and engage women on campus. WIHE seeks to increase the number of women in campus leadership jobs and provide a continuing source of education and passion on gender-related issues to leaders.

Your Notes

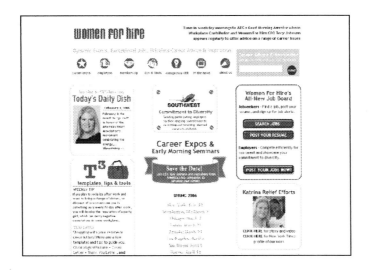

Women For Hire
www.womenforhire.com

Date Founded:	1999
Geographic Coverage:	International
Job Board:	Yes
Resume Database:	Yes
Job Agent:	Yes

Description: The first and only company devoted solely to a comprehensive array of recruitment services for women, Women For Hire offers signature career expos, inspiring speeches and seminars, a popular career-focused magazine, customized marketing programs, and an online job board that helps leading employers connect with top-notch professional women in all fields. Women For Hire offers advice, solutions, networking, tools, tips, and other career resources and guidance that will help women succeed.

Your Notes

Women in Neuroscience (WIN)
www.womeninneuroscience.org/classifieds/

Date Founded:	1980
Geographic Coverage:	International
Job Board:	Yes
Resume Database:	No
Job Agent:	No

Description: Women in Neuroscience (WIN) works to provide opportunities for women in neuroscience at all levels. Since its founding, WIN has played an instrumental role in providing the following services and programs to women neuroscientists: annual travel awards to the Society for Neuroscience (SFN) meeting, mentor/mentee partnering, quarterly newsletters, roommate referral service, and career development programs.

Your Notes

Women in Packaging, Inc.
www.womeninpackaging.org

Date Founded:	1993
Geographic Coverage:	International
Job Board:	Yes
Resume Database:	No
Job Agent:	No

Description: Women in Packaging, Inc. provides a forum for packaging education, networking and mentoring for the personal and professional development of women. The group also promotes and encourages the growth and success of women within the packaging industry. The Packaging Career Hotline is a great source for online job searching. This service of our organization provides many of the tools needed for a job search, including current job postings, resume service, coaching, articles, and expert advice from industry leaders.

Your Notes

www.weddles.com

Women in Sports Careers (WISC)
www.wiscnetwork.com

Date Founded:	1995
Geographic Coverage:	USA
Job Board:	Yes
Resume Database:	Yes
Job Agent:	No

Description: The mission of Women in Sports Careers (WISC) is to provide a nationwide network to serve the business and career needs of women with an interest in sports. Through its cutting edge technology, programs and services, the network provides an opportunity for women to grow their business, advance their careers, or simply grow professionally. Whether you are an entrepreneur, professional athlete, business or sports career woman, (or would like to be), this network may help you.

Your Notes

WomenSportsJobs.com
www.womensportsjobs.com

Date Founded:	1995
Geographic Coverage:	International
Job Board:	Yes
Resume Database:	Yes
Job Agent:	No

Description: WomenSportsJobs.com is a leading online career center for women in the sports industry and for women interested in sports-related fields. The site provides an online platform for connecting sports enterprises with the most qualified, career-minded individuals. Members have the ability to search hundreds of jobs in the sports industry, while employers can search a pool of qualified and diverse candidates. Jobs are posted daily to provide the most current and up-to-date opportunities in the industry.

Your Notes

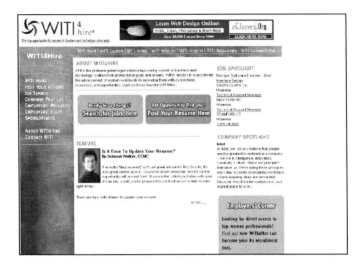

Women in Technology International (WITI)

www.witi4hire.com

Date Founded:	1989
Geographic Coverage:	International
Job Board:	Yes
Resume Database:	Yes
Job Agent:	Yes

Description: The mission of Women in Technology International (WITI) is to empower women worldwide to achieve unimagined possibilities and transformations through technology, leadership and economic prosperity. With a global network of smart, talented women and a market reach exceeding 2 million, WITI has powerful programs and partnerships that provide connections, resources, opportunities and a supportive environment of women committed to helping each other.

Your Notes

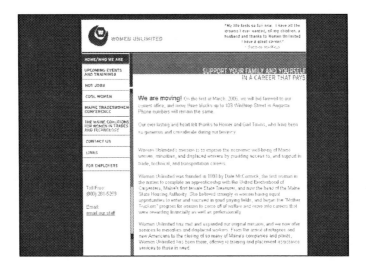

Women Unlimited
www.womenunlimited.org

Date Founded: 1988
Geographic Coverage: Regional-USA: ME
Job Board: Yes
Resume Database: No
Job Agent: No

Description: Women Unlimited's mission is to improve the economic well-being of Maine women, minorities, and displaced workers by providing access to and support in trade, technical, and transportation careers. We maintain a Job Bank with up-to-date employment opportunities. Over 100 employers contribute job openings. Women Unlimited also provides links to similar organizations throughout the United States.

Your Notes

www.weddles.com

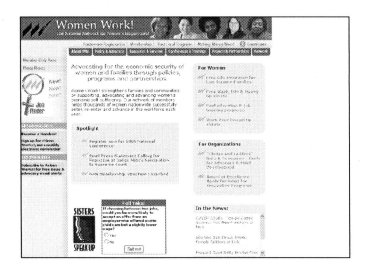

Women Work!

www.womenwork.org

Date Founded:	1978
Geographic Coverage:	International
Job Board:	Yes
Resume Database:	Yes
Job Agent:	Yes

Description: Women Work!, the National Network for Womenís Employment, is an organization that advocates for womenís economic security through policies, programs and partnerships. The Women Work! Job Finder allows job seekers to showcase their skills and work experience to prospective employers to find the best job opportunities, while others can take advantage of our networking, training and career development services.

Your Notes

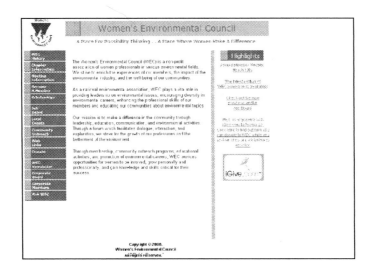

Womenís Environmental Council (WEC)

www.wecweb.org

Date Founded:	1993
Geographic Coverage:	Regional-USA: CA
Job Board:	Yes
Resume Database:	No
Job Agent:	No

Description: The Women's Environmental Council (WEC) is a nonprofit association of women professionals in various environmental fields. WEC strives to enrich the experiences of its members and the well-being of their communities. To that end, WEC plays a vital role in encouraging diversity in environmental careers, enhancing the professional skills of its members, and educating communities about environmental topics.

Your Notes

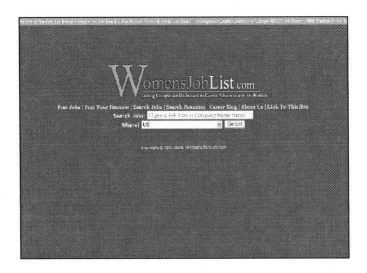

WomensJobList.com
www.womensjoblist.com

Date Founded:	2001
Geographic Coverage:	International
Job Board:	Yes
Resume Database:	Yes
Job Agent:	Yes

Description: WomensJobList.com combines the Internet's most powerful technologies into an elegant, powerful and easy-to-use system. This extraordinary recruiting tool facilitates communication between hiring officials and candidates like never before. Navigation is simple and provides visitors with a wealth of valuable information, quickly and easily. A combination of simplicity and elegance makes WomensJobList.com a useful resource for job seekers and recruiters alike.

Your Notes

www.weddles.com

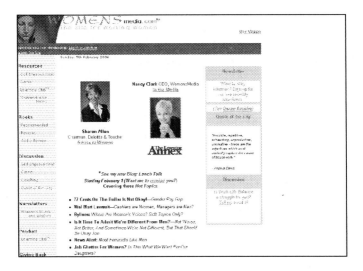

WomensMedia
www.womensmedia.com

Date Founded:	2002
Geographic Coverage:	International
Job Board:	No
Resume Database:	No
Job Agent:	No

Description: WomensMedia provides the latest in-depth material to help working women advance. We promote a positive attitude in women, a respect for womenís talents, and a way out of the cycle of seeing women as victims. The organization strives to help remove obstacles to women in business. The Career section of the site provides tools for making the most of a career, including articles on negotiation, balance, accountability, and response.

Your Notes

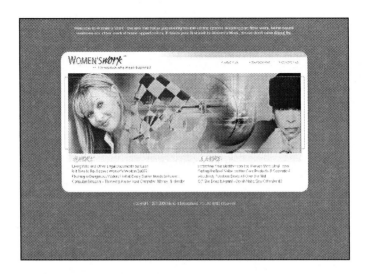

Women's Work
www.wwork.com

Date Founded: 1997
Geographic Coverage: USA
Job Board: No
Resume Database: No
Job Agent: No

Description: Women's Work is a site that helps women identify flexible career options including part-time work, home based business and other work-at-home opportunities. It offers a newsletter, career articles, and a Web log where users can interact with the site's founder. Started as a general business site, it has been redesigned to be a primary resource for women who are looking for a flexible career.

Your Notes

Work4Women

www.work4women.org

Date Founded: 1998
Geographic Coverage: USA
Job Board: No
Resume Database: No
Job Agent: No

Description: Work4Women provides tools, strategies and a virtual community to help increase womenís and girls' integration and retention in high-wage jobs that are considered nontraditional for women. Nontraditional occupations (NTOs) are jobs in which women comprise 25% or less of the workforce. The site includes job search resources for women looking for employment in nontraditional occupations, including links to job banks and articles.

Your Notes

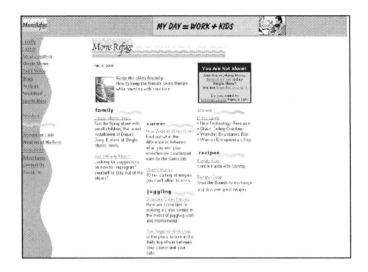

Working Moms Refuge
www.momsrefuge.com

Date Founded:	1997
Geographic Coverage:	International
Job Board:	No
Resume Database:	No
Job Agent:	No

Description: Working Moms Refuge was created by an impromptu community of working moms who wanted a place to connect and share tales, tips, and questions about balancing work and family. With an extensive career section that includes advice from a career coach, resources for the entrepreneurial parent, resources and job links for telecommuters, networking information, and general business articles, Working Moms Refuge is helpful to women who want to change or further their careers or need support juggling work and family life.

Your Notes

WorldWIT
www.worldwit.org

Date Founded:	2000
Geographic Coverage:	International
Job Board:	Yes
Resume Database:	No
Job Agent:	No

Description: WorldWIT (Women-Insights-Technology) is a leading global online and offline network for women in business and technology. WorldWIT provides resources to support the advancement of women at the intersection of work and life. More than 80 WorldWIT chapters around the world offer an unique blend of local networking and resources, as well as global connectivity. WorldWIT connects women with answers by linking them with 40,000 other women in business. Resources include a job bank and discussion groups.

Your Notes

www.weddles.com

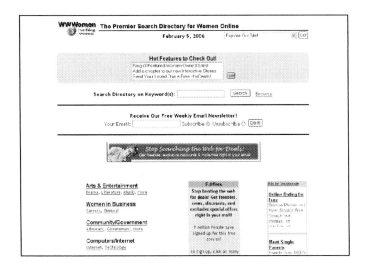

WWWomen.com
www.wwwomen.com

Date Founded:	1996
Geographic Coverage:	International
Job Board:	Yes
Resume Database:	No
Job Agent:	No

Description: WWWomen.com is a search directory geared towards women. The site includes a section on careers and general business issues where many links are offered. These links lead to a variety of Internet resources for women in various occupations, and women looking to change or further their careers. Also offered are discussion communities, advice columns, and newsletters.

Your Notes

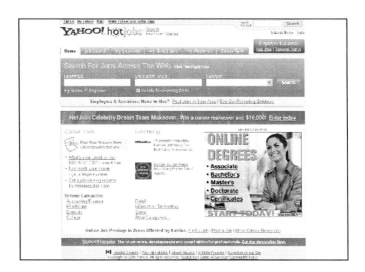

Yahoo! HotJobs
www.hotjobs.com

Date Founded:	1996
Geographic Coverage:	USA
Job Board:	Yes
Resume Database:	Yes
Job Agent:	Yes

Description: Yahoo! HotJobs provides job seekers with a full array of tools designed to help with any job search. Use our career tools to perfect your resume and improve your marketability, search our jobs database, and store your resume. Yahoo! HotJobs is the best solution for both job seekers and recruiters.

Your Notes

Yummy Mummy Careers

www.yummymummycareers.com

Date Founded:	2005
Geographic Coverage:	USA and Canada
Job Board:	Yes
Resume Database:	Yes
Job Agent:	No

Description: Yummy Mummy Careers is about maintaining a healthy balance in all areas of your life. Whether you are reassessing your career opportunities, looking for a position with a more flexible schedule or bringing your special talents back into the workforce, Yummy Mummy Careers is available to support and assist with your career goals. The site includes job listings, resume posting, and career advice.